- ADDRESSES -

For
Emergency
Occasions

Including:

**WELCOME ADDRESSES & RESPONSES,
DEDICATIONS, RESOLUTIONS,
TRIBUTES, OBITUARIES,
PASTOR'S ANNIVERSARIES, ETC.**

**R.H. BOYD PUBLISHING CORPORATION
NASHVILLE, TENNESSEE**

- ADDRESSES -
For
Emergency Occasions

© 1983

•

Revised 2001

•

R.H. Boyd Publishing Corporation
Nashville, Tennessee 37209-1049

Dr. R.H. Boyd, Founder
Dr. T.B. Boyd III, President/CEO

ISBN: 1-58942-016-0

Printed in the United States of America

- TABLE OF CONTENTS -

GENERAL WELCOME ADDRESSES

Welcome

With the psalmist we can say this (morning/afternoon/ evening), "I was glad when they said, let us go into the house of the Lord." We are glad to be in His house, and doubly glad (today/tonight) because we are in company with such sincere and enthusiastic Christians. We are glad that you have come to share this _____ program with us. You have bestowed upon us a great honor just by merely being here with us.

We know that you are always at home when you enter the house of the Lord, but be assured that in this house you are more welcome than ever. Our organization is looking forward to the inspiration you have planned to bring us, and I am sure much goodwill comes from our meeting together.

There are so many opportunities given us day after day. Today we feel that the Lord has sent you to us for a very special purpose — the opportunity to engage in worthwhile work for His sake and for His glory. Welcome to _____ Church, and may God bless every word spoken, every contact made, and every thought that has gone into the preparation of this wonderful occasion.

∽◌◌∾

Welcome

We of the _____ appreciate the interest you have shown by coming to our program this (morning/afternoon/ evening). We bid you welcome and hope that you will feel so at home that you will come back often to see us on other occasions. It is a pleasure to welcome our friends, for it is our friends who bring us our greatest happiness in this world of passing values.

Words fail to flow as I try to tell you how blessed we consider ourselves to have you present, but I hope before the (morning/afternoon/evening) is gone you will feel as happy and delighted to be here with us as we are to have you.

Welcome

This is indeed an honor, dear friends in Christ, to have you in our midst. We appreciate you taking time out from your many activities to join with us this evening. We know that you are busy doing many worthwhile tasks for our Lord, but God can always count on folks who are already too busy, to be about their Father's business at all times. Just your being here has shown to us that you have the same feeling for the Lord's house and the Lord's work as we do. We want to make you comfortable and entertain you so that you can say, "It has been good for us to be here. I'm glad we came." Welcome to _____. Welcome, welcome, welcome!

෴

Welcome

M _____ of Ceremonies, Pastor, Officers, and Members:

We welcome each of you on this happy occasion. We are so glad that you have come to be with us. We hope that your time spent here will be beneficial to you today, and throughout the future of your lives. It is a happy occasion for our group, and we desire to share this happiness with you throughout the program.

It is a great thing to have friends like you, for you are Christian friends — you share the same Christ, the same Lord and Savior whom we serve, and between us there is a bond greater than any earthly tie. Your presence here (today/tonight) encourages and inspires us to go on and to do more and more for our Lord and His wonderful kingdom enterprises.

I feel it an honor that I have been chosen to welcome you. The pastor and our _____ (organization) join with me in giving you a hearty welcome which we hope will last until that glad day when Jesus our Lord throws open the doors of heaven wide and bids us to enter and sit down with Him in His kingdom forevermore!

෴

Welcome

Master of Ceremonies, President, Other Officers, and Friends:

When we were making plans for our program, it was our desire to include all of our friends. We wanted each of you to be present to enjoy the atmosphere of our new building with us. We are so very grateful to you for your interest in this, your neighbor church, and we appreciate the little and big contributions from you all which have helped to make it a reality. We appreciate your presence here to rejoice with us and to share in our great (day/night).

Let me assure you that you are welcome (today/tonight) and any time that you would like to worship with us. We feel that the Lord has greatly blessed us and we want you to share in our blessing, and to feel at home whenever you pass through our portals. Thank you again for being with us in body and in spirit. It is our heart's dearest wish that you may receive a blessing for coming (today/tonight).

❧☙

Welcome

Master of Ceremonies and Friends:

We want you to know the joy in our hearts (today/tonight) as we survey this wonderful group of Christians. The joy in our hearts is full and overflowing! It is good to have you in our church, and we want you to be as happy to be here as we are to have you. It is good to have our friends with us to share our Lord's house. To be with friends is the nearest we can get to heaven in this world, and so ours is a heavenly joy.

We are glad you have come to be with us for this celebration. Now you know we welcome you and hope you will benefit by our program.

❧☙

Welcome for the First Meeting of the New Year

This is the first of a New Year. We are setting out on a journey of which we can have no knowledge in advance. The road is one on which we have never traveled before. We know not what any day in the year _____ will bring to us, what our duties will be, what burdens shall be laid upon us, or what sorrows we may be called upon to endure. How can we know the way? As we sit in the quiet this first evening and ask the question, we hear an answer that is full of comfort — Jesus says to us, "I am the Way." All we shall have to do is to stay with Christ in _____ (year). He has made a way through the world for us. He has a definite way for each of us to go.

(Today/Tonight) I welcome you into a New Year, into the first meeting of _____ (year) and I am glad that you are here for the first service. May it be an inspiration to you down through all the weeks and months of 20____, and may it be a challenge to you all the years of your life to follow Jesus Christ, "The Way, The truth, the Life."

☙❦❧

Address of Welcome

Master of Ceremonies:

We do not propose, in welcoming you, to worry you with a lengthy address of meaningless words; but we hope to make you feel the warmth of our hospitality, and to make your sojourn with us a source of pleasure and spiritual happiness.

Anticipating your coming for several weeks, our minds have been busy, thinking and planning to that end, that your coming to us on this grand occasion would be one of your fondest and most delightful visits.

Today, our hearts overflow with an inexpressible joy because you are here. Being one among this generous and hospitable group of Sunday school scholars, I have been selected to give you words of welcome.

The superintendent, officers, and teachers of our great Sunday school, joined by our honorable pastor, support me in telling you that you are welcome—not because it is an age-old custom to say this, but because our every heartbeat is motivated and propelled by the spirit of gratitude for your presence here.

8

In the 133rd Psalm we read: "Behold, how good and how pleasant it is for brethren to dwell together in unity." The psalmist's meaning is that it is delightful when those who are united by blood live together in love and harmony. Primarily, this was to the children of Israel; but it also means us — the "Spiritual Israel" united together in the bonds of Christian love by the blood of Jesus Christ, which hath made us one in purpose, one in our objectives, and one in determination. Therefore, we all come to the hill of Zion today, as the seat of holy worship to the God of Abraham, Isaac, and Jacob.

We welcome you here, because, and in like manner, for the tender and loving thoughts you have of us and for us, and for the inspiration you bring.

We welcome you to share with us Christian fellowship, brotherly love, and unstained friendship rooted in long happy years of our cooperation.

We welcome you because your only flag is the blood-spattered Banner of the Christ of Calvary, made so by the purple stream that flowed from His wounded brow, feet, hands, and bruised back; who in spite of His agony, misery, and sufferings, declared, "For this purpose came I into the world, and to this end was I born; If I, be lifted up, I will draw all men unto me."

We welcome you because you believe in the Lord Jesus and bear in your bodies the mark of self-sacrifice and burden bearing, and therefore, "Your witness is in heaven and your record is on High."

ഛൊൊഌ

SPECIAL WELCOMES

Welcome to Women's Regional or District Meeting

Mistress of Ceremonies, (or Madam President and Officers):
We welcome you here today to the _____ Church and pray that your desired goals may be reached in this meeting held within the confines of our church. We want you to know how very

9

welcome you are, as you are truly the women who build and never destroy, the women who spread happiness and never gloom, the women who make character and never pull it down!

Life affords many opportunities for service, and I feel that this great women's organization convening here today is an opportunity to serve our Lord in spirit and in truth. In Galatians 6:10 we read, "So then, while we have opportunity, let us do good to all men, and especially to those who are of the household of the faith." We know that you plan only for the good that you may do, and we welcome you here because our community and our world needs such faithful Christian doers of the Word more than any other kind.

It is wonderful to see the way the door of opportunity swings open before us. There are those who would do great things, but because they wait for greater opportunities, life passes them by and the acts of love and kindness pass them by, and one day the door of opportunity is shut and sealed. But not so with active faithful Christian women such as you are — you are God's candles, shining forth as lights in the world, holding forth the Word of life.

There is no action so slight or so mean that it may be done to a great purpose and ennobled thereby, nor is any purpose so great but that it may be helped much — most especially, the chief of all purposes, the pleasing of God. You, as Christian women builders, are getting rich returns here and now for your efforts in the service of our Lord and Savior Jesus Christ, and we want you to know you are appreciated.

We welcome you and assure you of a continual welcome throughout our great meeting.

ﾟﾟﾟ

Welcome to Pastor's Anniversary Service

We, the members of _____ Church, have been blessed for _____ years under the inspired and efficient leadership of our beloved pastor, Reverend _____ , a man of God who has led us wisely and well. Now when we come to the celebration

10

of his _____ anniversary as pastor of _____ Church, it is with hearts filled with joy and thanksgiving that we welcome our members and friends to share with us the glowing memories of Rev. _____'s service. It is with the hope that a portion of our happiness and praise may overflow into your hearts that we welcome you here on this momentous occasion. The love that we feel for our pastor is deep and genuine and reaches out to encircle the hosts of friends gathered here to wish him well. We pray the leadership of the Holy Spirit upon our guest minister (or guest speaker) as he challenges our hearts with a message from on high.

We are encouraged by your presence, and thrilled by your participation in this anniversary program, and extend to you a permanent welcome to worship with us on all future occasions.

ぐゐひ

Response to Welcome for Pastor's Anniversary

We have heard your gracious words of welcome on this great anniversary occasion, and we thank you for the genuine hospitality that you have extended to us on behalf of your pastor and congregation.

We anticipated just such a welcome as we approached your hospitable church — we saw the evidence of welcome in your smiling faces as we entered, and now we feel the sincerity of your welcome through the cordial words just spoken. We have come (today/tonight) to share this happy occasion with you and to congratulate your pastor upon his wonderful church family. And we trust that we may be mutually benefitted by this great spiritual feast.

ぐゐひ

Welcome to Woman's Day Service by the Pastor

Mistress of Ceremonies, Directors of Woman's Day Activities, and Friends:

Today it is with a great deal of gratitude that I welcome to our church and community this inspirational group of ladies who

11

have served their churches in every possible capacity to further the work of Christ's kingdom. You are the leaders in our churches, the very backbone of all organizations. We daily realize how little we could do without our consecrated Christian women members and workers. It is an honor to have you in our church, and to greet this great gathering of the so-called "weaker sex." Surely when it comes to missions, evangelization, care of children, visitation in the homes, ministry to the sick — you are far from being the "weaker sex!" We do welcome you and pray for you as you seek to raise womanhood to the high level of purity, service and achievement on which she was placed by the head of the church, Our Lord and Savior, Jesus Christ.

✿

Response to Welcome to Woman's Day Service

To the Pastor, Mistress of Ceremonies, Chairman of Woman's Day Activities, Friends, and Co-workers:

We thank you for your very gracious welcome on this wonderful occasion of your Woman's Day Service. We are grateful for your hospitality and kindness to us in inviting us to share this great day of the year with you. Our earnest prayer is that we may always keep Christ first in all our plans, as you have done today, and that we may ever work together as women who seek to bring in the kingdom of Christ here on earth.

✿

Welcome to District Sunday School Congress or Other Group of Christian Workers

To adult workers, Junior teachers, Home and Extension Department leaders, musicians, ministers, Intermediate leaders, BTU directors, and to all who represent any branch of religious education, we welcome you on behalf of our great city and church. We assure you we are indeed grateful for the opportunity of playing host to so fine a group of outstanding Christian experts and specialists.

We feel humble that you have chosen our church for such a great and glorious gathering. We love our church and know that the Lord has blessed us in an unusual manner in providing a way to build and grow. We are inspired by your very presence, and our hearts are open to receive the message you will share with us as servants of our Lord. The Christ in us salutes the Christ in you, which ever Ensures a hearty welcome among Christians.

The entire church and its facilities are yours to use while you are our guests: we want you to be comfortable and to enjoy your stay with us that it may be engraved upon your hearts as a bejeweled memory that will glisten more and more as days go by. I hope you will feel free to call on any of our members to help you in any way you may need assistance.

_____ Church has looked forward with great anticipation to this hour because we have heard of your abilities and talents which are invested in the cause of Christ. We knew it would be a spiritual feast for us to have you here where we all might benefit by your lectures, teaching, speeches, sermons, and music. Let me assure you on behalf of the pastor, the Sunday school, and the B.T.U. of the _____ Church, that you are welcome — indeed, you are twice welcome — no, thrice welcome to our midst!

❦

Welcome to WCTU Convention or Meeting

Mistress of Ceremonies, Pastor, White Ribboners from Everywhere:

We want you to know how pleased we are over your presence here (today/tonight). Our welcome is very deep and heartfelt, for those who stand for the cause of purity, morality, and abstinence are ever welcome here.

Life brings us many opportunities to serve. We feel that the Woman's Christian Temperance Union is an opportunity for us to serve our Lord in manifold ways as we promote alcohol education, teach respect for law and the value of total abstinence for the individual, and encourage and solicit pledged members who,

13

through organization and department functioning, will carry forward the work of Miss Frances Willard. We are glad that you are here to wage war against beverage alcohol, which is undoubtedly the nation's greatest deceiver, the most persistent and efficient wrecker of homes, and a merciless defamer of character. We welcome you to this gathering where we know you will stress the need for trained Christian leadership, especially for lecture and demonstration work with youth. We are with you in your efforts to urge cooperation with law enforcement agencies everywhere so the traffic in beverage alcohol may become less accessible.

Your badge of honor is a white ribbon, and we welcome any wearer of the white ribbon of purity, which signifies membership in one of the greatest, most courageous movements among women in our land, the Woman's Christian Temperance Union.

Welcome Address to Sunday School Workers

Master of Ceremonies, Pastor and Friends:

"Study to show thyself approved unto God, a workman that needeth not to be ashamed, rightly dividing the word of truth" (2 Timothy 2:15). (Today/Tonight) it is my privilege and profound pleasure to welcome you and to congratulate you on the work you have done for the advancement of our program here at _____ Sunday school. I am sure at times it has seemed that you have taken on more than you felt you could do; but as you look back on your years of labor and see the eternal good you have wrought in the lives of young people, and realize what you have accomplished in them for the glory of God, you will feel that every effort was worthwhile, and you must experience a deep satisfaction over the fact that you have invested all your talents in this great task.

We of the _____ Sunday school do welcome you here (today/tonight) and hope that we can show some appreciation to you for your accomplishments and hard work, in the name of Jesus.

14

Welcome for District or State
Women's Meeting or Convention

Madam President, Sisters and Friends:

Dear Sisters in Christ, we welcome you (today/tonight) to this precious sisterhood in Christ Jesus. We want you to realize how grateful we are to you and others like you who serve so fervently in the missionary interests of our Lord's kingdom from day to day. While we women realize that the Christian's field is the world, we also know that our responsibility begins in our own community. "But ye shall receive power, after that the Holy Ghost is come upon you: and ye shall be witnesses unto me in Judea, and in Samaria, and unto the uttermost part of the earth" (Acts 1:8).

The local Christian woman, more than anyone else, has the responsibility of reaching the unchurched and the unsaved in this area. If we fail, then how shall they learn of our gracious Lord and Savior, Jesus Christ? The Lord Jesus gave a clear and emphatic commission to His church to go into all the world and preach the Gospel to every creature. We welcome you into this great missionary fellowship (today/tonight) that we better fulfill this great commission with your help.

The grace you Christian sisters have experienced will be a powerful incentive for you to make that grace known to others. We welcome you to this gathering, for we feel that through this program all Christian sisters will be prompted by love and gratitude to carry out the world-embracing mission that Christ gave to all who would follow Him.

You ladies have shown us that the highest purpose of your lives is to share the love of Christ Jesus with all people. "Ye are the light of the world," said Christ. We welcome you because you are light to a dark world. "Neither do men light a candle, and put it under a bushel, but on a candlestick, and it giveth light unto all that are in the house. Let your light so shine among men that they may see your good works and glorify your Father which is in heaven." Because we feel that you are sincerely striving to shine through good missionary works, not for your own glory but for the glory of God, we welcome you. You are welcome here because you serve the Lord. That He may ever bless you, and through you bless others, is our prayer for you.

⚬❦⚬

Welcome Address for Our Pastor's Aid Auxiliary

Mistress of Ceremonies, Ladies and Gentlemen:

This very unique and cordial affair to which you have been invited is sponsored by a group of earnest, faithful, and interested members of our church. These members have set out to do something worthwhile to help encourage, inspire, and strengthen our pastor in arduous and trying responsibilities as the leader, pastor, and head man of our church.

We feel that the true leader, Gospel preacher, and pastor of any church is truly worthy of all joys, happiness and provision that life can afford. We feel that he who is the shepherd of our church is deserving of any and every good thing. This organization happily accepts the task of helping to make this sure.

Your presence here is deeply appreciated. It tells us in silent language that you are in sympathy with us, that you endorse our effort, and have come here to encourage and help us in this laudable cause.

Few of God's true ministers are ever wholeheartedly supported by those to whom they administer. Too often, they are neglected and made to share the short end; and yet untiringly they press forward, under orders from Him who called and sent them, to be thou faithful unto death.

Our desire in this and other efforts is to have our pastor smell the sweet aroma from the flower of our gratitude, taste the nectar from the cup of our generosity, and feel the power of our love through what we do for him while he can realize them all.

We are deeply eager for each of you to enjoy every moment here with us. And believe it when I tell you that your presence is definitely a contribution to this affair for which we are grateful.

⚬❦⚬

16

Welcome to Student Union Retreat
or Any BSU Meeting

This is indeed an honor for our church and congregation. This occasion will be long remembered because it has been looked forward to for so long. To have students who own the name of Jesus Christ as our guests for a little while is an answer to our prayers. For many years I have attended these meetings, watched you as you made your great plans, observed the training you were receiving, and then followed through to see many of you go out into the world to live the true Christian life for which you had received the incentive at BSU meetings.

(Today/Tonight) in our midst, we have the future leaders of our churches, the missionaries, the preachers, the teachers, the officers, superintendents, and soul winners of our nation. There is one here to fill every office — yes, it is a glorious night for _____ Church.

You have on your shoulders a great load; but with the help of our heavenly Father great things can happen. It will be up to you, and you, and you to answer the needs around about you. It is a great challenge, one that you are facing as you finish your schooling. Remember the words of Paul, "I can do all things through Christ which strengtheneth me."

By entering into such close and loving relationship with Christ you will unconsciously reproduce His traits of character. By meditating upon His life as revealed in His Word, and by imitating His example in going about doing good, you cannot fail our Lord.

As you enter into your great fellowship on the eve of this retreat, we welcome you and hope you will feel at home. It is a great honor to have you, and may we serve you in any way possible while you meet with us at _____ .

May God bless each of you and lead you into the field He has chosen for you.

Welcome to Special Meeting of Brotherhood Union

To all the Laymen Assembled for This Special Occasion and Their Friends:

This is a momentous evening to have in our church, and we rejoice to see so large a number of brothers in Christ gathered together to do Him honor and to learn more of the responsibilities that they as laymen in the church have had placed upon their shoulders.

You Christian men realize that the greatest need in our world today is Christian influence. This is a gigantic responsibility that faces you — to use your influence at all times for Christ and the church. But, remembering the words of Paul—that we can do all things through Christ who strengthens us—we know you can measure up to this great task; for you are well equipped through His power.

Through the saving grace of Jesus Christ there is created within the layman's heart a sense of deep gratitude which impels him to use his influence as Jesus wants it used in every association of His own people and with businessmen in all walks of life. There is no limit, Christian brethren, to the opportunities that a Christian has in our day along these lines, and that the church has in acting as the center of our work. You men can wield your influence at your work, in factory, in office, at places of amusement, at vacation spots, while traveling, and in all circumstances of life.

We are aware of the achievements you have made already to further the Lord's work, and we pray that (today/tonight)'s gathering may enable you to reach more and more men for Christ. Hence, we bid you welcome as one bids all who come in the name of the Lord Jesus. We are glad that you are here, and we thank you already for doing us good. Your very presence makes us happy, and your contribution in speech, lecture, and song will make us even happier. Welcome to _____, O men of the Brotherhood Union.

Welcome to a New Pastor and His Wife

This is a long-awaited occasion in the life of our church, one that will always be remembered as a red-letter day in the history of our organization as we welcome our new pastor and his wife and family into the fellowship of our church.

We have looked forward to this moment when we miay take into our hearts and homes the man we feel God has sent us to be our pastor and leader, the shepherd of our flock.

On this occasion we pledge to you the wholehearted cooperation of every member and every auxiliary of our church, to the end that souls may be won for Jesus Christ, our Lord, and that those who are Christians already may reach a higher, nobler plane of living because of your spiritual influence, counsel, and preaching. We welcome you, your gracious wife, and your _____ children to the fellowship of _____ Church to be our pastor until God has other plans for you.

இலூ

Welcome to Visiting Choirs

Master of Ceremonies, Pastors, Visiting Choirs, Ladies and Gentlemen:

When we began working toward this great meeting some time ago, we wanted to include all the wonderful choirs of our city. (Today/Tonight) our great goal has been reached and realized. In our midst we have representatives of _____ churches and approximately _____ voices — voices that are continually being used in service for their Lord; for the words of the hymns you sing so harmoniously week after week carry their message straight to the hearts of the listener as emphatically as do the words of a sermon.

(Today/Tonight) we have all ages with us — our junior choirs — may they continue to raise the sweet fresh voices of youth enthusiastically to God in praise and worship — our older groups and senior choirs who sing with the deep resonance of experience and faith which glorify our services from week to week.

19

You have used your talent to tell His wonderful story in song. Everyone loves to sing, and you have led those who do not have such melodious voices to want to sing His praises too.

We are glad that you have come and we want you to feel at home. The songs that will be sung (today/tonight) are familiar to us all. Because we are together in Christ (today/tonight) they will mean more than ever to us. We welcome you, boys and girls, men and women, to this great and glorious gathering of musicians. May you sing like nightingales — and like nightingales, give God all the glory!

✆👀

RESPONSES TO WELCOME ADDRESSES

Response

Friends and Associates:

On behalf of the guests here assembled, I receive and accept your beautiful words of welcome with much pleasure, first, because of the happy spirit in which they were extended; second, because they come to us as an expression of love and appreciation for our presence here.

I assure you that we will treasure your choice words and long feel the warmth of the hospitality and fellowship so impressively made in your fine welcome.

Already, since being in your presence, we have been inspired. Our minds have been given much food for thought. The very fine way you have carried on this great affair bespeaks the sincerity of the magnanimous spirit that fills your hearts.

My earnest hope is that you will continue in this good way of giving encouragement and inspiration to the people. I congratulate you and bid you Godspeed in the successful accomplishment of the glorious task set before you. You are yet in the ascendency of your meridian height. Continue to press your claim with a self-determination naught but death can stop, and more glorious success will reward you ere the day is done.

20

I thank you for the honor given me in responding to the address of welcome, and for your patience and most friendly reception.

❧◎◎☙

Response

As you were speaking, we felt that you must be psychic, for you have said just the words that make us feel welcome indeed. We do appreciate your warmth and cordiality. Our hearts are filled to overflowing because we feel the presence of our Lord here (today/tonight) in this wonderful gathering.

Our sincere hope is that we may bring some inspiration that will draw you even closer to our Lord and Savior Jesus Christ.

❧◎◎☙

Response

You have said just the right words to ensure us we are truly welcome here. On behalf of _____, I want to accept your heartfelt welcome address. We are indeed grateful to you for allowing us to share with you this great occasion.

We are here to share your fellowship and are happy that you have made such a meeting possible and have included us in it. But that is just like you at _____ Church, for you have a "heart as big as the universe," and we are grateful to have a small part of it.

We have already enjoyed your great singing and are proud to be counted among your many, many friends. It is good to be in _____ Church!

❧◎◎☙

Response

The fellowship we feel here within these hallowed walls is good for us; we feel drawn very close to your great organization and are happy to be among your group. I feel that words are inadequate when I try to express my gratitude to you for our cordial welcome. But may I say in my feeble way, "Thank you" for including us on your great program and in your list of guests.

⚜

Response

Your heartfelt greeting makes our hearts glad. We appreciate all the kind words and the wonderful welcome you have given us this evening.

We are grateful to you for inviting us, and we hope that when we leave you, you will feel that you have received a blessing from the words that we have to say, but most of all from the Christ which we carry in our hearts. You are very kind and very cordial. Your kindness and cordiality are deeply appreciated.

⚜

Response

We are assured of our welcome here (today/tonight), for you have already shown us your hospitality and we feel humble before the deep friendship you offer us. We feel that the bond between us has already been strengthened. We shall remember these soul-touching words and for days to come will be glad, ever glad, that we came to your gathering (today/tonight).

We are interested in your church as we are in all churches that work hard for the founder of the church, Jesus Christ our Lord. We are grateful to be here and grateful for your words of welcome.

⚜

Response

Master of Ceremonies, Pastor, Officers, Members and All Our Congenial Hosts:

Thank you for your kind welcome — we feel that you mean just what you say after such meaningful prayer, as prayed by Brother _____. I know our groups join me in saying, "It is good to be here, and we are glad that we have come."

We do feel this evening that we are in the midst of Christian friends, and we feel keenly the fine spirit of this great church. As we entered your church (today/tonight) we felt an atmosphere of reverence, and we join with you in praising our Lord and Savior, Jesus Christ.

We wish you well in all you do in _____ Church to enlarge the kingdom of God. With such fine leaders and workers as you have here (today/tonight), I have no doubt that you will accomplish great things in the Master's cause.

Thank you again for your kind invitation and welcome. We shall pray to God for your continued growth.

‿◦◎◦‿

Response

We, the members of _____, are indeed grateful to you (today/tonight) for your invitation to such a special occasion and the opportunity to share in its happiness. Your prayers and your songs have been an inspiration to us already. It is with sincere gratitude that we accept your welcome.

In your greetings you have just shown us your love — not for self, but for God and His children. We bask in that love as flowers bask and bloom in the sunshine.

You have shown your courage by holding forth the Word of truth and ever moving onward for God's kingdom.

You have shown your faith — sincere faith in God and His word, by following your usual custom of long-range planning and then carrying through to the desired outcome.

You have shown us your joy — the joy of the Lord is our strength, and this joy attracts others out in the world who do not know the happiness of being safe in Jesus.

We are happy Christians (today/tonight). As we worship with you throughout the rest of your program, I pray God's blessing upon every word spoken and everything that is done. May it be done to the glory of God.

‿◦◎◦‿

Response

Mistress of Ceremonies, Ladies and Gentlemen:

It has become my pleasant duty to accept these words of welcome, and I find that I am at a loss as to what to say after so eloquent an expression of Christian love and hospitality.

In my humble manner I express to you our thanks for having been invited and for being included on your list of Christian friends for this most inspirational occasion.

I bring greetings from _____ Church and want to invite you to worship with us at your very first opportunity.

If our presence has been of any encouragement, we are happy. We feel that we are truly the benefactors (today/tonight), and we are happy to share in this fine gathering.

I feel that all things, great or small, can be accomplished if we only trust in our Lord and work together. Your church is a living example, and we are proud of you. We have only to be in your midst for a few moments to feel the sincere love and mutual appreciation you have for one another. May God bless you in this hour and through all the days, nights, weeks, months and years to come is our prayer for you!

❧❧❧

Response

Master of Ceremonies, Pastor, Visiting Friends, and All of Our Charming Hosts and Hostesses:

We have a feeling (today/tonight) that we are indeed among Christian friends, and are sure of our welcome. We felt that we were invited because you wanted us to share with you your good fortune. I am sure each of us will be greatly benefitted by your presence here, and we are assured that God must be pleased as He looks down upon His children and sees the fine spirit in which they are sharing the blessings of His work.

We all know our duties and responsibilities as Christian men and women, but so often we have to be reminded that we are not quite fulfilling them to the best of our ability. God does require of us that we do our best. God is so good to us to give us another chance after we have failed him so many times. We, in this community, are blessed with our churches and the fine Christian members we have in our congregation to make this a happy, growing, harmonious neighborhood.

You set before us an example (today/tonight) that I hope each of us can follow in our daily lives. We are indeed grateful to you, brother Pastor, and friends, for allowing us to come into your hearts and to be a part in this great movement for Christ.

ɷ

DEDICATIONS

Dedication of New Church Library

"Of the making of books there is no end," says the sage. We are thrilled (today/tonight) at the _____ Church to survey the goodly collection of books that we can consider a part of what we hope with God's help will be the church's continually expanding library. Through the earnest efforts of our Library Committee (name them) and the special gifts of _____ (name those who have made unusual contributions of books or money gifts) we see a dream realized that has long been in the hearts and minds of our Sunday school workers and leaders. We rejoice that at last we can invite our young people to read some of the most wholesome stories that have ever been written. We fondly cherish the hope that there will be a love of good literature fostered in the minds and hearts of our membership that will last as long as life lasts, through the ministry of this library. We have chosen to call this the _____ Library in memory of our dear departed _____ (name), who was one of our staunchest loyal leaders and Bible teachers. We trust that you all will avail yourselves of this great library from time to time and abide by its rules as to withdrawing and returning books. The services of _____ (name), who has consented to act as church librarian this year, will be at your disposal. You will find the hours of library service listed on the door, and you are cordially invited to enter, to browse around at your leisure, or to take the book of your choice home with you whenever you wish.

This library is dedicated to the glory of God. The books in it are chosen because they are on that high plane of living and literature that will make them appropriate for Christians of all ages.

∽◉∾

The Dedication of a New Home

There can be no happier occasion in which Christians are invited to participate than that which dedicates a new home to the welfare of the family and the service of God. We pray (today/tonight) that this home may be the focal point for this Christian family, and not merely a place in which they hang their hats.

From the basement to the attic may it be filled with the presence of God. May its foundations be built upon truth and righteousness, its walls shut in love and happiness, shut out hate and prejudice. May its furnishings be the fruits of the spirit — love, joy, peace, longsuffering, gentleness, goodness, faith, meekness, temperance — against which there is no law. May the very sidewalks that lead to the entryways of this home remind the members of this family of the walk in the Spirit. "If we live in the Spirit, let us also walk in the Spirit."

May the bathroom of the house remind the family of the cleanliness required of God, which is called "next to godliness," and may it not stop at the thought of physical cleanliness only, but go on to the purity of speech and deed that makes man acceptable to God through Jesus Christ.

May the living room ever remind them of the Creator, who first gave each living soul life and breath, and may they be constrained to live for Jesus Christ at all times. May they invite into their living room friends and companions who honor God. May the literature on their magazine tables include the Word of God, the Book of the Ages and such periodicals as will lift them toward God because of their Christian content.

26

May the kitchen house a happy housemaker and mother who does her cooking, dishwashing, and similar mundane tasks as unto the Lord, recalling at all times as she works therein that it is the Lord above who has given her strength to work, and may she praise Him for it.

May the dining room of this home ever be a reminder of the Living Bread, which God sent to sinful man in His Son, Jesus Christ, who taught man that he cannot live by bread alone, but by every word that proceeds from the Father.

May the bedrooms ever recall that while God "giveth unto His beloved sleep" night after night throughout his life, there are those who are denied this privilege through ill health or diseased minds, and let them not forget to praise God for this precious gift of sleep. May they ever remember that the rest that refreshes them upon their beds each night is but a type of the everlasting rest that God has promised to all faithful souls.

May even the hallways of this house, if there be any, remind you that life is but a passage between rooms in God's great universe and to traverse them with reverence and to fill each day of our present life with service and honorable deeds for His name's sake, that we may be presented at the last gate, the last doorway, in worthy manner to stand before the Master Builder, the Master Carpenter in whose hands lies our eternal fate. May the lives lived in this new home be acceptable as they build them day by day by the words they speak and the deeds they accomplish. Let harmony, truth, and love ever reign throughout these rooms; may none in this family ever go to bed with malice or resentment burning in his heart one for the other.

May every room in this home be a room of prayer — where the busy person or the idle may feel free to waft a message to that listening Ear on high and know that he may be heard.

⋇

The Dedication of a New Organ

From the time that the gentle shepherd-musician played upon his harp to ease and calm the troubled mind of King Saul, music

27

has been employed by the servants of God to bring comfort, calm, and worship into the minds of the faithful. Later in David's career, when he returned from the slaughter of the Philistine giant, Goliath, he was met by the women of the cities of Israel who greeted him with songs of joy and hymns of praise with instruments of music.

In our church worship services we have had need for some time of a new organ which could enhance the spirit of our members in worship and which would turn our services into a place "like the garden of the Lord's" where "joy and gladness shall be found therein, thanksgiving, and the voice of melody." Today we see our dream realized as we sing in harmony with the swelling chords of our new _____ organ. It is the gift of the members of the sacrificing congregation to the house of God. (Here mention any special donors who have perhaps made appreciable gifts for the purchase of the instrument).

We are appreciative of the unusually beautiful music played this morning by our organist _____ and congratulate him (or her) upon his (or her) early mastery of so fine an instrument. Our hearts are lifted up with praise as we view this shining and beautiful instrument of music, and we praise God for making such an addition to our auditorium possible. We pray that its ministry may reach out and gather into our folds many unenlisted souls who are in search of the God we serve, that they may know as we know the God of all beauty, whose music is the voice of many winds, of millions of raindrops, of oceans of water beating their waves upon the shores. Let us consecrate this organ to the worship of God, that we may unite in singing His praises. With each hymn we sing, accompanied by this instrument of beautiful chords, let us think of the words the hymnwriter intended as sermons in music. May they lift our thoughts heavenward in adoration of the God of all the earth.

May the ministry of this new organ sink deeply into our lives as we sing with new fervor to its accompaniment each Lord's Day:

> Just as an organist takes a few rich notes
> And builds upon them symphonies that rise —

A glory of high melody which floats
Upon the air to make earth a paradise —
So on life's sure, deep chords our hands shall press;
A brave symphony our soul shall play,
So we may write a song of godliness
Into the simple scale of every day.

∽◉◎∾

The Dedication of New Church Pews

Beloved Members of _____ Church:

Today, through the continuing gracious goodness of a loving heavenly Father, we are privileged to view the finished pews that have been in stalled throughout our auditorium (chapel, worship center, etc). Due to the generosity of our members and the sacrificial giving of our officers, deacons, and Sunday school leaders and workers, our dream of several years' standing has been realized, and today we view with pride and pleasure these shining objects which are products of the carpenter's art. Our Lord Himself was a carpenter and might often have had a part in the finishing of pews or ceremonial seats which appeared in the synagogues of His day. It is in His memory and to His service that today we dedicate these pews.

How can we show appreciation for these costly new pews from week to week? How can we ensure their continual enhancement of our worship service Lord's Day after Lord's Day, for sitting in them, week after week, and being permitted to take a part in the worship service for which they have been built, bought, and installed?

To show proper appreciation the worshippers must have the proper attitude toward the worship services of this church. Do not sit stiffly and severely as if daring God to get anything by the door of your heart. Relax, as you sit in these shining pews. Surrender to the worship mood. As you sit in these pews, Sunday after Sunday, try to observe these six rules which should govern the attitude and actions of all those who sit in pews everywhere in the worship of God:

29

1. Never miss the service. Never let your pew be empty. That is fundamental. Occasional church-going is like occasional practicing on a musical instrument. It never gets beyond the stage of painful awkwardness. Come to the service regularly, sit in your pew on time, and you will enter a glorious stage of freedom.

2. As you sit in your pew, study to know the worship pattern. The pastor can help you. Each organization of our church would profit much by setting aside an evening for a special study of worship from the pew sitter's viewpoint. For joyous church-going know the service and the meaning of each part.

3. Be receptive, not critical, as you enter your pew. Face the panorama of spiritual values which a church service brings you like you would watch a sunset or listen to music. Be receptive. "Incline" thine ear. Surrender yourself calmly to the glorious experience and respond deep within yourself or vocally if need be, to express the joy you feel as you sit in the pew of a Christian church in a free land.

4. Do not expect the sermon to please you every time. No pastor can please every member with every sermon preached. If so, the message would be compromised. Even in human relationships, Jesus commented, "beware when all men speak well of you." You may sit in your pew expecting comfort and strength, but sometimes we need to be stabbed awake spiritually or morally. It is when a sermon hits you as you sit in your pew that God is getting something across to you.

5. Give as well as receive, as you sit there in that pew. There are many ways you can contribute: tithes and offerings for the Gospel work of the congregation, at home and in the mission fields. The mission fields are supported by sitters in pews, in cities and towns and villages of our lands, and you as a pew-sitter can send your love and prayers across the ocean to those who do not know Jesus as Savior and Lord, through the gift you make from your pew.

6. Tell others what you have seen and heard from your pew. Tell them the things that will bring blessings and help when they did

not come to sit in THEIR pews, God only knows why. If you would keep the blessings of worship — share them. Say to your neighbor over the fence — "the anthem was so helpful, the message so fine, and the prayer brought us close to God." If you have prayed in your pew, your face will be radiant when you leave the pew behind.

Pew-sitting need not be boring; it can be a spiritual adventure. Make the most of this privilege today while it is still yours. While our pews still have the sparkles of newness upon them, let us make the pledge that they shall never be empty, and that those that are empty today will be filled with new workers or unenlisted friends and visitors week after week, through our renewed efforts in behalf of our Lord's church. We call upon God today to bless these pews and hallow them, that through them many souls may find their way into His saving power and into His church.

❧❧❧

General Dedication

Today, we gather around this which through God's goodness has come at last into our possession. We thank God for it and pray that it may be used entirely for His glory. If there be any ulterior motive of selfishness, covetousness, or materialism in our hearts as we survey it with pride, may they be dissolved now forever. As we stand before God proud of this _____, we now dedicate it to His glory, His service, and His church. May it ever be a reminder to us of the goodness of God, of many unmerited favors that He through his grace has bestowed upon us. May we be ever mindful that not of our own strength have we gotten this precious _____, which we have long yearned for, but that "every good gift and every perfect gift is from above, and cometh down from the Father of lights, with whom is no variableness, neither shadow of turning" (James 1:17).

❧❧❧

RESOLUTIONS

Resolution

"Blessed be the God and Father of our Lord Jesus Christ, which according to His abundant mercy hath begotten us again unto a lively hope by the resurrection of Jesus Christ from the dead. To an inheritance incorruptible, and undefiled and that fadeth not away, reserved in heaven for you, Who are kept by the power of God through faith unto salvation ready to be revealed in the last time" (1 Peter 1:3-5).

> I will believe, though all around be darkness,
> Believe to see the rainbow after rain;
> Believe that light will surely follow darkness,
> And frozen earth will yield her flowers again;
> I must believe, He hears my faintest call —
> For Jesus lives and reigns, and God is over all.

In His own way and for His own purpose, God has reached down into our garden to pluck one of our fairest flowers. On _____ (date) He called the spirit of our dearly beloved member _____ (name) home to be with Him throughout eternity.

Whereas, we the officers and members of the _____ (organization) desire to express our love and respect to our departed member, we make these resolutions, a copy of which will be kept in our records, a copy sent to the press, and a copy given to the family with our deepest sympathy.

Whereas, there is no adequate way in which we may express our deep appreciation to our late member for her unfailing loyalty and her countless contributions to our _____ (organization), and in view of her sincere and unselfish life of ministry, which has been an example of womanly modesty and Christlike love, we thank our gracious Lord and Father for her and for her influence for good which has been like a benediction from above.

The cause of youth was dear to _____'s heart, and the problems of youth were real to her. She took a vicarious interest in all their trials and helped countless young people to find their way toward noble living and higher ground. She always sought to stimulate the growth of a missionary spirit and missionary interest among the women of our church and community and busied herself much with personal evangelism and soul winning. The encouragement she gave to new converts was the expression of the Christian, sisterly love she felt toward them, and her great desire to promote the work of her heavenly Father whom she sought to please in all things.

Mrs. _____ felt that with immortality glowing before her, her brief years on earth should be marked by earnestness, reverence, love, and faithfulness, and she was true to this belief in all that she said and did. We know that Sister _____ is far better off today, for the translation of a Christian life from earth to heaven is but the removal of a tender plant from a cold northern garden, where it is stunted and dying, into a tropical field, where it puts out most luxuriant growths and covers itself with splendor. So we would not wish her back, in our selfish grief, but pledge ourselves to cherish her memory and to emulate her life of Christian devotion and service.

Humbly submitted, _____ .

❦

Resolution

Whereas, God has called from his home and dear family _____, who passed from labor to reward and to a land far fairer than ours on _____ (date) and

Whereas, _____ has served in _____ Church for so many years and

Whereas, our wise heavenly Father has taken a true worker of His to be with Him in a land more beautiful than he has ever known and

Whereas Brother (Sister) _____ served his church and friends hard and long, and his life radiated his love for his Master

33

and his faithfulness to his fellowman. He loved his church and was always there when he was needed. We feel that his influence for living a true Christian life in the hearts of his friends and co-workers, as long as they shall live and

Whereas Brother _____ has left behind him a memory fragrant with good deeds. He would concur with the following thought, were he here in the flesh today:

"I shall not fear

Death's dreaded voice to hear,

I shall not fear the night

When day is done;

My life was loyal to the light

And served the Sun."

Be it resolved, therefore, that the sympathy of our _____ (organization) be extended to _____ (family/spouse). May the Lord continue to watch over you is our prayer and may the precious memories of your loved one, which "bless and burn" keep you ever on the road that leads to God.

Signed— Pastor / (or other officer)

⋘◉⋙

Resolution

Our _____ (organization) suffered heartfelt loss in the death of our member _____ (name) who was so dearly loved and respected by all with whom she associated. Her life was above reproach and so lived that others came to know Christ as their Savior as she had known Him intimately, joyously, radiantly. Her loyalty to her church and her kindness to those less fortunate shall always be a living memorial to her. Especially shall we miss her praying for us. To hear _____ pray in public or in small special groups was a benediction upon all those who listened. _____ crowded into her life the lovely, unselfish, and helpful things that showed her love for Christ and for her fellowwomen. We are better people today because we knew her. Her prayer must have been, as she faced death:

"Oh, may I join the choir invisible
Of those immortal dead who live again
In lives made better by their presence."

Humbly submitted,
Organization President/Secretary

⁓⊙⊙⁓

Resolution

"And the city lieth foursquare ... and the gates of it shall not be shut at all by day: for there shall be no night there" (Revelation 21:16, 25).

He sendeth sun, He sendeth shower;
Alike they're needful for the flower;
And joys and tears alike are sent
To give the soul fit nourishment;
As come to me, or cloud or sun,
Father, Thy will, not mine be done!

Can loving children e'er reprove
With murmurs whom they trust and love?
Creator! I would ever be
A trusting, loving child to Thee:
As comes to me or cloud or sun,
Father, Thy will, not mine, be done!

Oh, ne'er will I.at life repine!
Enough that Thou hast made it mine:
When falls the shadow cold of death,
I yet will sing with parting breath:
As comes to me or shade or sun,
Father Thy will, not mine, be done!

Whereas, God has called from our midst Brother (Sister) _____ a faithful member of _____ Church, and

Whereas, the (organization) hopes that these few inadequate lines may in some way comfort the bereaved family.

35

Resolve, that a copy be sent to them, with our sympathy and the prayer that God may sustain them in so deep a loss.

⌘

Resolution

"I give unto them eternal life" (John 10:28).

We, Christian friends, have the promises of God that death, which people fear most, shall be to us the most blessed of experiences dependent only upon our perfect trust in Him. Death in unclasping earth's tawdry treasures; it is by breaking out in the desert; the heart comes to it blossoming time!

"Strength"

Lord, make me strong!
Let my soul rooted be
Afar from vales of rest,
Flung close to heaven upon a great rock's breast;
Unsheltered and alone, but strong in Thee.
Lord, plant my spirit high upon the crest
Of Thine eternal strength!
Then, though life's breaking struggles come at length,
Their storms shall only bend me to Thy breast!

Resolved, a copy of these resolutions to be sent to the family of the deceased, with our sincere and deep-felt sympathy.

Sorrowfully submitted, _____

⌘

Resolution

"There remaineth therefore a rest to the people of God" (Hebrews 4:9). Heaven will be sweeter and more beautiful, more to be desired because of the entrance through its shining gates of your loved one who left this earth on _____ (date) at _____ o'clock.

Let us think of the last and sweetest homecoming in the Father's house of many mansions, where our dear ones are waiting for us. May the blessed Lord come into our hearts more completely, and may we rest our weary souls on Him. "Blessed are the dead who die in the Lord" (Revelation 14:13).

Therefore, be it resolved:

1. That the family of the deceased that they have our lasting and heartfelt sympathy;

2. That we thank God for the life and witness of _____ (name) and who has lived among us;

3. That a copy of these resolutions be sent to the family and to the press.

Resolution

"Whosoever liveth and believeth in me shall never die" (John 11:26).

We thank Thee, for our dear friend and faithful worker of the Lord, whose truth, integrity, and beauty of spirit is enshrined in our hearts. One by one Thou dost gather the scattered families out of the earthly light into heavenly glory, from the distraction and strife and weariness of time to the peace of eternity.

We thank Thee for the labors and the joys of Brother _____, who passed away on _____ (date) at _____ o'clock at his home, in the presence of his dear ones. May His family live together in Thy faith and love, and in that hope which is the forerunner of immortality.

Let all who are sad take heart again;
We are not alone in our hours of pain,
Our Father stoops from His throne above
To soothe and quiet us with His love.
He leaves us not when the storm is high,
And we have safety for He is nigh;
Can it be trouble which He doth share?
Oh, rest in peace for the Lord does care.

Resolution

Resolution by the _____

Whereas: God in His great power has removed from our midst our true Christian friend.

Resolved: that in the homegoing of this our dear one we have lost a noble worker and a tireless leader and our _____ will feel keenly his absence for a long time to come.

Resolved: That we express the deep sympathy we feel personally and collectively to his dear ones, and may they rely for comfort upon the gracious Lord of heaven and earth;

Resolved: that our church has been a better place because _____ came to be with us for a while and blessed us by his presence and sweet winning ways of service.

Resolved: that a copy of these resolutions be sent to the family, a copy kept in our minutes, and a copy sent to the press.

"Is anything too hard for the Lord? Dwell within his light through the waiting-time; drink in deeds of His gracious Spirit, the Comforter; and thou weary heart, shall be used to breathe influences that shall be sweet and blest through eternity; thy memory shall be fragrant even when thy place is known no more."

Respectfully submitted, _____

❧

Resolution

We, the _____ (organization) have suffered a deep loss in the home-going of _____ who was ever faithful and a dependable member of _____ . She was always on the alert to help her fellowmen, and her influence will live long to be felt by those who were encouraged, helped, and cheered by her advice, friendship, and counsel.

The _____ has lost a noble character, but God has promised in His great Book, "I will not leave you comfortless, I will come to you" (John 14:18).

He has always kept His promises and if His followers will lean upon Him, He will guide them all the way.

38

The valley may be dark, the shadows deep,
But, O, the Shepherd guards His lonely sheep,
And through the gloom, He'll lead me Home.
My Heavenly Father watches over me.

Be it resolved, that our deepest expression of sympathy be extended to the family of the deceased, whom we commit unto the God of all comfort, who will sustain them in their hour of loss.

Sorrowfully submitted, _____ (organization)

∽❦∾

Resolution

Whereas, the _____ Church has suffered a great loss in the homegoing of _____, who was loved by all who knew her (him).

Whereas, she lived a true Christian life and has served her Lord well. Her loyalty to her church, her faithfulness to her family, and her kindness to her friends shall ever be a living memorial to her beautiful life. She has labored hard and long and the Lord has promised her rest.

Whereas, Sister _____ departed this life _____ (date) at _____ o'clock and will no longer go about her accustomed duties, we mourn, not as those who have no hope, but as those who expect to meet with her again in that other world beyond the horizon.

Therefore, be it resolved, that we strive to emulate her beautiful service-filled life in every respect; that we express our sympathy to her sorrowing family, and present them a copy of these resolutions, with the reminder that Jesus, the Man of Sorrows, understands all that transpires in human experience and that he said, "Come unto me, all ye that labor and are heavy laden, and I will give you rest" (Matthew 11:28). Also our Lord said, "Blessed are they that mourn: for they shall be comforted" (Matthew 5:4).

∽❦∾

Resolution for a Faithful Member
of a Woman's Organization

Whereas, again a human spirit has taken its flight at the call of the heavenly Father to the mansion prepared for her from the foundation of the earth by an all-wise and loving God, we pen these resolutions to express our grief in the loss of our faithful member and friend _____ .

Whereas, the _____ (organization) has lost a fine loyal member and the world has lost a noble character in the passing of Mrs. _____, we rejoice that her belief in the promise of God in Psalm 73:24 is now fulfilled. "Thou shalt guide me with thy counsel, and afterward receive me to glory."

Her daily life gave evidence of the fact that she believed God's Word and followed His guidance, seeking His leadership in all that she said and did. She was upright, loving, and kind in all her ways, sincere and genuine in all her doings. She has left behind her a beautiful memory, and we pray that young people may emulate her life.

Therefore, be it resolved:

That, even as we mourn _____'s passing, we are resigned to the all-wise heavenly Father's will;

That we express our gratitude to God for having left this beautiful life among us for a time to blossom out and bless us with its sweetness and righteousness, like the fragrance of a rose;

That we express to the family and relatives who grieve today our deep sympathy in their loss and the reminder that their loss is heaven's gain;

That a copy of these resolutions be placed in our secretarial record and a copy sent to the family of the deceased.

Humbly submitted, _____ (organization)

కుండా

Resolution for a Lodge Member or Club Member

This morning the call of the heavenly Father to another human soul has come to carry him away to that mansion prepared for him from the foundation of the world by an all-loving God, and we pen these resolutions in the memory of _____ to express our grief and loss in the passing of our faithful club member and friend.

Whereas, the _____ Club (or other organization) has lost a fine, loyal member and the world has lost a great Christian character in the passing of Brother _____, we rejoice that, in the midst of grief, we are assured that his passing has brought him eternal joy and fellowship with God, for he has received the crown of righteousness laid up for all the faithful. He was patriotic, dependable, devoted to the principles for which our Club stands, and was sincere and genuine in all his doings. He has left behind him a beautiful memory which well might be emulated by the young.

Therefore, be it resolved:

That even as we mourn _____'s going away from us, we are resigned to the will of an all-knowing, kind heavenly Father;

That we express gratitude to God for having shared with us for a short time the life of _____, with its beautiful principles of service and noble living;

And that we express to the family and relatives who grieve over their loved one's loss this day, our deep sympathy and the reminder that on God's calendar, these trials and crosses are but for a moment:

> But for a moment the trials and crosses,
> Weariness, trouble, and tears.
> When we have passed through the valley of shadows,
> Then, oh, what glory appears!
>
> Glory outshining the sun in its splendor,
> Glory outweighing earth's gold.
> After the moment of our light affliction
> Glory eternal, untold.
>
> Joy, like the sunrise, will come in the morning,
> Sorrow and sighing shall cease;
> Moments are passing — then life everlasting,
> Filled with eternity's peace!

"But for a moment" to patiently trust Him —
Wait till the shadows are passed.
"But for a moment," look up and take courage —
Faith will bring visions at last.

Humbly submitted, Signed _____ Club

⏤⊙⊙⏤

Resolution for a Man Who Has Been Very Active in Christian Work

Whereas, it has pleased our heavenly Father to transfer from the labors of this life to the sweet rest and fellowship of the saints in heaven our dearly beloved brother in the Lord, Mr. _____ and,

Whereas we, the members of the _____ (organization) desire to place on record our love and esteem for his life and labor; and in view of his noble and sincere testimony which has been an example of Christian manhood and devotion to the kingdom's cause, we thank the heavenly Father for him, and feel that we should express our sympathy to his wife, son, and daughter, as well as other relatives and friends.

When we thank the Lord for the privilege of having known this fine and spiritual personality, who was so interested in God's work that he was in attendance at all of the services of his church and enjoyed the full privileges of its membership. He prayed faithfully for his church and his pastor gave them his faithful support at all times.

Whereas from _____ (date) when he first allied himself with the _____ (organization) until _____ (date) when the Lord called him home, Mr. never ceased to show an active interest in the program of this organization. (Mention offices he held.) He was ever willing to do his part and cheerfully assumed any responsibility which was his.

Whereas although he was ever willing to serve, Mr. _____ never sought a place of prominence. He did everything requested of him as unto the Lord, but his spirit of genuine humility followed the example of his Lord, making him willing to

42

do the humblest tasks as well as important ones, doing both well, yet not seeking recognition for the same. It was with real regret that Mr. _____'s failing health caused him to remain away from our _____ for some time before his death, but he had made such an indelible impression upon our organization that we never ceased to consider him a full member, and his interest in our program never waned. We never ceased to miss him in our regular meetings, but we have rejoiced to know that he was under the tender care of his own during his last illness.

Whereas Mr. _____ truly loved his Lord, serving in many Christian capacities, and it is a small wonder that his unselfish and cooperative nature made for him many friends. It was with a sense of shock and real loss that the news of his death came to the many friends and co-workers who had learned to love him in _____ (organization).

Be it therefore resolved: That though his presence will be greatly missed by his loved ones and those to whom he had endeared himself in our organization, that they accept the Christian submission to God's will, His calling our beloved brother Mr. _____ home. To his devoted wife, son, daughter, and other relatives and friends, we extend our heartfelt sympathy and commend them to the Divine Comforter who is able to sustain, encourage and strengthen all who call upon Him.

Resolve further, that we will ever cherish his memory and emulate his admirable traits, and look forward with joy to meeting him in the home which he knew for so many years was being prepared for him in the glory land. "Precious in the sight of the Lord is the death of His saints. For whether we live, we live unto the Lord; and whether we die, we die unto the Lord; whether we live therefore, or die, we are the Lord's."

Lovingly submitted, (Board of officers of the _____)

❧❀❧

Resolution on Behalf of a Church Auxiliary on the Death of a Member

We, the officers and members of the _____ of the _____ Church, in sincerity extend our deepest sympathy to

_____ in this hour of bereavement, caused by the passing of _____ .

In the passing of _____, we sincerely recognize that we have lost a faithful member, our church an ardent and devoted laborer, and our community a warm and sympathetic friend.

He was a soul of good humor, speaking words of encouragement and urging us to higher and nobler ideals. By his kindly disposition and unselfish dealings with his associates, he endeared himself to all the memory of which will be a worthy monument to his life.

He was a Christian. In his private life, his actions were open to the same scrutiny as his public career. In this he has furnished to the young men an example for great service.

> Jesus Saviour, Pilot me,
> Over life's tempestuous sea,
> Unknown waves before me roll,
> Hiding rocks and treacherous sheol,
> chart and compass, come from thee,
> Jesus Saviour, Pilot me.

Be it resolved that we, the members of _____ bow in humble submission to the will of God, and commend the bereaved family to Him who sees all and knows every heart; and entreat them, "Console yourselves in the hope of a reunion, so that after life's remaining ills are past, it is like healing oil to the wounded heart, comforted with pleasing thoughts rather than sad."

Be it further resolved, that we enter sympathetically into the sorrows of the bereaved, and bid them hope, through the master of all life, that they shall see their loved one again, for the last enemy that shall destroy us is death.

Then, we shall meet with the loved ones gone. We shall know as we are known, some sweet day "by and by."

Humbly submitted, _____

President_____/Secretary

Resolution on Behalf of an Organization When a Prominent Person Has Passed

When one has given his (or her) life for a good cause, bestowing freely and unselfishly his (or her) talent, influence, and time for the betterment of the community in which he lives, touching all phases of the religious, social, and civic life of the people, death is momentous.

We pause here today, to pay our last respects to our departed friend, associate, and neighbor, who departed this life _____ (date). We can say, without fear or contradiction, that in the passing of this deceased a pure sweet soul is at rest. A full day's work finished, being weary of the burdens of life, the God whom he served so devotedly sent down from the shining courts of glory a beautiful glorified messenger with orders to release from its suffering, decaying body, racked with pain and agony, a Christian spirit, a sanctified soul that has long been imprisoned in its house of clay and caused a sleep of which only God knows the awakening.

How carefully then should we live, knowing that some day we too, must pay the debt that he has paid. We are living in a world where solemn shadows are continually falling upon our pathway; shadows that teach us the insecurity of all temporal blessings and warn us that here, there is no abiding stay.

The death of _____ again emphasizes that none is superior to the last call, which is common to all beings. Again we are reminded that the way of man leads through the grave, and they who walk with the master here shall not tarry in the grave, but shall be led gently on into the land of light and beauty.

"Friend after friend departs.
Who hath not lost a friend?
There is no union here of hearts,
That finds not here an end."

Our beloved friend has fallen in life's battle, acknowledged the supremacy of death, yielded to a victory that no one can resist, and entered upon a complete rest. It was decreed in the beginning,

45

"all must die"; but we shall rise from death to everlasting life if we are faithful unto death in the cause of Christ.

Therefore, be it resolved, that we share every sorrow of the bereaved family and extend to them our deepest sympathy, and that we stand always ready to welcome them to the cross, for earth hath no sorrow that heaven cannot heal.

Be it further resolved, that a copy of this resolution be given to the family and a copy be sent to the press for publication.

Sorrowfully submitted, _____

⁓෨෧ꔷ

Resolution for a Young Christian

The mysterious angel of death has visited our church again and taken from our midst _____, a young Christian but true to his belief.

Whereas, God in His infinite wisdom and mercy, has removed _____ from us, we are better because of our brief association with him (her);

Be it resolved: That we extend to his dear family our deep and sincere sympathy in their great loss, and may they rely heavily upon their heavenly Father for comfort to sustain them in this hour of grief. God's ways are past finding out, but there is always good in them for those who trust Him.

A little hand stole softly
Into my own that day
When it needed the touch that I loved so much
To strengthen me on the way.
It seems to say in a strange, sweet way,
"I love you and understand."
And calmed my fears as my hot tears
Fell over that little hand.
Perhaps there are tenderer, sweeter things
Somewhere in the sun-bright land
But I thank God for His blessing
In the clasping of that little hand.

Be it resolved: that a copy of this resolution be sent to the family of this little one, with our deepest sympathy, and a copy be held for the minutes.

_____ Committee

❧

Resolution for a Young People's Worker

Whereas on the morning of _____ (date), the death angel came into the home of _____ and plucked for his garden another lovely flower.

Whereas she became a Christian at an early age, and joined the _____ Church, being baptized by Brother _____ on _____ (date). She began serving the Lord immediately upon joining His church, and through the years has been a faithful, ardent, loving worker among our young folk, helping them to make decisions concerning their life work. Throughout the world there are many of them whose hearts are bowed in sorrow at the thought of this early friend they have lost.

"The Lord gave, and the Lord hath taken away: blessed be the name of the Lord" (Job 1:21).

To the family we say, if you will cast all your sorrow and care upon Him, you will never be alone. These dear ones who are gone from us are not lost, but they are gone to rest a little sooner than we have been privileged to do. Peace be to that bed of dust where they are hidden, by the hand of their God, from unknown dangers, sickness, sorrow, and trouble.

❧

TRIBUTES

Tribute to a Pastor

Rev. _____'s homegoing has been a great shock to our church and community. He was a true servant of our Lord Jesus Christ and a great preacher, "rightly dividing the word of truth."

47

He faithfully preached the Word of God and sought ever to preach the whole counsel of God, which necessitated many hours of Bible study and memorization.

He was our pastor, shepherd, and counselor; he reproved and rebuked but ever in a spirit of love. He cared for the sick and the sorrowing, and in his community they were never neglected. Those in trouble knew him as a friend who was always to be counted on, and he was always alert to be wherever he was most needed in these capacities.

He was a missionary; his crowning virtue was his faithfulness in testimony. His life was an example to his church members, his fellow ministers, and all who knew him. He considered himself expendable for his people and the cause of Christ.

He worked in love, wisdom, humility, with courage, patience, joy, and self-denial. Only God could have enabled him to serve as he served. His motto seemed to be:

"Give me, Savior, a purpose deep,

In joy or sorrow Thy trust to keep

And so thru trouble, care and strife,

Glorify Thee in my daily life.

Only one life, 'Twill soon be past;

Only what's done for Christ will last."

&loves;

A Tribute

_____'s sudden going has caused a great sadness. She was a faithful Christian leader, true to God's Word and loyal to her church and friends. She knew the true meaning of friendship and never counted the cost of loyalty. There are many in her immediate surroundings who weep today, for they have lost the best friend they ever had.

She was a Christian whose light shone like a million stars, and her light will linger long after her body has disappeared from our vision, through the lives she has touched round about her.

Sister _____ lived, prayed, and witnessed for her Lord in her daily life.

John 1:7, "The same came for witness, to bear witness of the Light, that all men through him might believe." John's purpose in life was to witness, and as _____ lived, she had the same purpose because she had found salvation and wanted to lead others to the joy and satisfaction of a Christlike life.

Her life was dedicated to His glory. By faith, her entire life and purpose was transformed: she was "alive unto God." Her body was God's temple and her heart the Spirit's workshop. May others meditate upon this beautiful life and seek to emulate the beauty of character and testimony ever displayed by our departed Sister _____.

e⊙⊙ꜱ

A Tribute

_____, who passed away on _____, served faithfully her church and her community. She placed her body, mind, soul, and possessions unhesitatingly at God's disposal without any reservations.

She invested all her life for God and dedicated her whole life to God's glory. Her life work spread from her home, into society, into the community at large. As a member of the church, her testimony was always constructive and faithful.

The love of Christ, and for Christ, was the mainspring of her life. Her heart had but one throne, and Christ sat upon that throne. Christ was her all in all; she had...

a heart through which God loved,

a voice through which God spoke,

a hand through which God helped.

Her whole life was dedicated to God. We shall miss her, but we pray that another will be inspired to carry on in the work of the Lord as she did so fervently.

e⊙⊙ꜱ

A Tribute to a Worthy Person Taken by Death

As far as we have any knowledge, man is the only one of all God's created beings to whom is given the information that all earthly life must end in death.

The experience and observations of mankind early in life impresses upon man's mind the fact that death is the common lot of all races.

Of all beautiful things in life, the most beautiful is character. He who possesses a beautiful character is worthy of notice. A beautiful life is the fruit of a beautiful character; he whom we memorialize here at this time possessed a beautiful character and lived a beautiful life. He died a beautiful death. He of whom I speak, is the late _____.

To my mind the highest tribute that can be paid to any man is that he was loved by his fellowman. Truly, this is the sentiment of all who knew this gallant and noble Christian gentleman and noble citizen, _____, our friend, big brother, and civic leader.

With a lasting gratitude for his exemplary life, his tireless and unselfish labor among us; the good he did, the things he taught, and the inspiration we imbibed; we dedicate this hour. He was a hero for God, possessed with the Abrahamic type of faith, filled with the spirit of his Christ. He was a friend to all, free from deceit, and met all with a kindly smile.

He was a hard worker. He sought to help and encourage all who needed such. He was always busy, and ever alert to find something to do, or a word to encourage.

Steady grind and constant work wore down his body. His physical strength weakened, and affliction fell upon him. Tired and weary, he took to his bed. There patiently, yet often in pain and misery, he waited, happily and good natured, on the orders from his Christ, whom he served so devotedly. On _____ (date), his spirit-filled soul took its flight across death's stream, where at this moment he rests from his labor; but his memory will ever live in the hearts and minds of us who knew him.

OBITUARIES

Obituary

The angel of death has visited again at _____ Church and taken from our midst Brother (Sister) _____. He joined the church and was baptized _____ (date) and has been a faithful member of _____ Church for _____ years. He lived at all times in keeping with the high standards set for him by his Master. He received his education at _____ and _____ and served as _____ (position held) for years. He was married at _____ (location) to _____ (spouse) in _____ (year). From this union was born _____ children who have followed him in Christian profession and conduct. We shall miss him, for we all loved him, but heaven loved him best.

✢

Obituary

Brother (Sister) _____ was called home on _____ (date). He was converted at the age of _____ and joined _____ Church. His leadership as _____ (position held) will always live in our church through the lives of those he taught and worked with in the Lord's service. To his family we express our sincere sympathy, and in the words of John's gospel, we say, "Let not your heart be troubled," for he is not dead, he is just away.

✢

Obituary

Brother (Sister) _____ passed into the great beyond _____ (date) to be with the Lord and Savior Jesus Christ. Brother _____ was a faithful member at _____ Church. He joined _____ Church at the age of _____ and was baptized by Brother _____. He served his Lord

51

well and he will be greatly missed. He was a good neighbor and many counted him a friend.

Our hearts are filled with sorrow, but we realize that this homegoing is the greatest experience of Brother _____'s life, which was filled with wonderful experiences as he was a worker with God.

Brother _____ had a favorite passage of Scripture that he was often heard to quote, and now in his memory we quote it here, as he sweetly rests today in the care of the Good Shepherd:

"The Lord is my shepherd; I shall not want. He maketh me to lie down in green pastures: He leadeth me beside the still waters. He restoreth my soul: He leadeth me in the paths of right-eousness for his name's sake. Yea, though I walk through the val-ley of the shadow of death, I will fear no evil: for thou art with me; thy rod and thy staff they comfort me. Thou preparest a table before me in the presence of mine enemies: thou anointest my head with oil; my cup runneth over. Surely goodness and mercy shall follow me all the days of my life: and I will dwell in the house of the Lord forever."

❧❦❧

Obituary

A godly life ended _____, 20____ (date) when _____ was taken from us. We know he is at rest with our heavenly Father. After so much suffering by Brother (Sister) _____, the Lord took from him all pain and took him to Himself, where there is no pain and no burden of a tear.

There are three steps to heaven — out of self; into Christ; into Glory.

Brother _____ took these first two steps in life and lived a beautiful life in Christ. Now he has taken the third step where there is no more weeping, no pain, no sorrow, no disap-pointment. We know he is satisfied now and that he is reaping his great reward reserved for the faithful.

His enthusiasm for his religion, his willingness to pay the price, and to do his best for his Lord was his life purpose. It made him a radiant and happy Christian.

He now has fulfilled that purpose and his friends and family, though they may weep awhile, should rejoice with him, and thank our heavenly Father for the life he lived among us, and for taking him to the land of Glory as He has promised all the faithful.

∽✺∾

Obituary

"For me to live is Christ, and to die is gain," said the apostle Paul. We know that this would be the message if our dear Sister _____ were able to give us a message today from the portals of heaven where she has gone to be forever with the Lord. It is said that Fanny Crosby, the great hymn writer, on her death bed said, "How can anyone call it a dark valley? It is all light and love!" Then, stretching her arms out to Christ, she whispered, "I could run to meet Him."

The dear Christian woman whom we memorialize today must have felt the same way, for she loved her Lord and always wanted others to know Him.

To his Thessalonian friends Paul wrote, "I would not have you to be ignorant, brethren, concerning them which are asleep, that ye sorrow not, even as others which have no hope" (1 Thessalonians 4:13). Hope of what? What possible hope can bring comfort at such a time as this when we mourn the passing of so dear a woman, so great a leader?

In "the first dark days of nothingness" or still darker days which follow, listen, and thank God with all your heart for every word from the Scriptures, "For if we believe that Jesus died and rose again, even so them also which sleep in Jesus will God bring with him" (1 Thessalonians 4:14).

The dear face, for the sight of which we hunger, shall look on us again; the voice that has left this world so tuneless shall once more bless our ears; we shall see our loved one again and be with her forevermore!

> So long Thy power hath blest me,
> Sure it still will lead me on,
> O'er moor and fen, O'er crag and torrent,

53

Till the night is gone.

And with the morn those angel faces smile,

Which I have loved long since, and lost awhile.

⋲⊙⊙⊙⋺

Obituary
"'Tis Life Beyond"

I watched a sail until it dropped from sight
Over the rounding sea — a gleam of light
A last, far-flashed farewell, and, like a thought
Slip out of mind, it vanished and was not.

Yet, to the helmsman standing at the wheel
Broad seas still swept beneath the gliding keel;
Disaster? Change? He left no slightest sign,
Nor dreamed he of that dim horizon line.

So may it be, perchance, when down the tide
Our dear ones vanish. Peacefully they glide
On level seas, nor mark the unknown bound.
We call it death — to them 'tis life beyond.

Yesterday one we loved and knew stepped across the threshold that we call death, but it was only a step into another room, and not a stepping out of the fellowship of life. It was but a stepping into one of the other rooms of our Father's house. The noises of the world make it hard for us to hear the still small voice beyond the door; the world's bright lights blind our eyes to the soft glow of eternity; the constant concern with material things deadens our sensitiveness to the spiritual values of that unseen land until we are tempted even to deny their reality.

_____ (name) is at peace with God now, and rejoicing in her happy heavenly home.

We must not mourn as those without hope, for _____ has gone to get the great reward promised to all who faithfully serve our Lord and Savior Jesus Christ.

    _____ was born about _____ years ago in _____ County. In _____ (date) she was married to _____. To this union _____ children were born. To her family she was loving and faithful, striving always to keep them happy and in material comforts of life. She reared her children in the fear of the Lord and aided many others to come to know Jesus as their personal Savior and Lord. We commend the family to the love and compassion of our kind heavenly Father. "Wait on the Lord; be of good courage, and He shall strengthen thine heart" (Psalm 27:14).

⌒◉◟

Obituary

"Some day," we say, and turn our eyes
Toward the fair hills of Paradise;
Some day, some time, a sweet new rest
Shall blossom, flower-like, in each breast;
Some day, some time, our eyes shall see
The faces kept in memory; Some day their hands
shall clasp our hand, Just over in the Morning-land.

    A loved friend has departed from this earth for another land. "A city which hath foundations, whose builder and maker is God" (Hebrews 11:10).

    Yes, earth grows the poorer, heaven seems more desirable when a loved one has gone into the shadowland. Shadow, did I say? Here is the shadow. There the light blots out the radiance of the sun. Dark with excess of brightness that higher world is because our eyes are so weak, our faith so dim. In this ever-changing world of phenomena we seem but a shadow pursuing shadows, like the rest. When we reach there we shall know the truth, that love and life were the only real things we have ever found.

So, _____, our dear one, who has gone on before us, we sorrow, but not as those who have no hope. We sorrow because we shall miss your kindly smile, your helpful ways, and your encouraging spirit.

Mrs. _____ (or Miss, Mr., etc.) closed her eyes in her last sleep on _____, 20_____, at _____ o'clock in _____ (place). Mrs. _____ was born and reared in _____; came to _____ (town), was married to _____ (spouse) on _____ (date). To this union was born _____ children. She was converted _____ (date) and joined the _____ Church on _____ (date). She served in _____ (positions or offices held).

She worked faithfully and long, so let us praise God that she has, along with all other tired laborers, found in God a place of rest. Let the family of our dear friend be comforted, for your loved one is only sleeping and will awake in a land of rest. All that God does for His children He does in love and for their benefit, so we commend you to God who will sustain and strengthen you in your great loss.

∽∾∽

Obituary

Without warning death plucked a flower from our garden on _____ (date) and Sister (Brother) _____ was called from earth to heaven's reward. She was born in _____, joined _____ Church at the age of _____, and was active in all church auxiliaries. She invested her many talents into every broadening, good work she could find. She was active in church societies, ever ready to do what was needed, always on the alert as to how she could help, comfort, and cheer someone more sad or lonely or needy than herself. Every minute of her day she filled with helpful, absorbing works. She visited the sick and the sorrowing, sewed and made garments for the needy, taught in the Sunday school, and won many young hearts for the Master. Her life was full, rich, and happy. She loved people and sought to help them; she loved her Lord and sought to please Him. It will be hard to find someone to fill the many places where she served, but we ask God's guidance in this, as we express to her bereaved family the deep heartfelt sympathy that we feel for them in her loss.

∞⊙∞

Obituary

Into another of our Christian homes death has again entered with his unrelenting face, his unhearing ears, his sealed lips. Again a family has gone close to the valley of the shadows of death and left a loved one there—they to turn back to the earth, life desolate, burdened, heartbroken; and the deceased to step into the heaven of life, where there is no more death, neither sorrow, nor crying, nor pain. Surely we cannot grieve for our dear Brother _____ who was called home to be with his Lord on _____ evening. It is for ourselves we mourn, forgetting perhaps, in our selfish sorrow that "it is well" with our beloved in that better country.

> Angels of life and death alike are His
> Without His leave they pass no threshold o'er,
> Who, then, would wish or dare, believing this,
> Against His messengers to shut the door?

"For if we believe that Jesus died and rose again, even so, them which also sleep in Jesus will God bring with Him ... wherefore comfort one another with these words" (1 Thessalonians 4:14-18).

∞⊙∞

Obituary for a Faithful Deacon

On the morning of _____ (date), the angel of death came into the home of _____ and with chilly fingers sealed the lips of our faithful and devout deacon, Brother _____. For _____ years he was a member of this church and for _____ of those years he served as a faithful deacon of our deacon board.

When _____ years of age, Deacon _____ became a Christian, being baptized at _____ on _____ (date) and joining the _____ Church. Since that time he has spent many fruitful years in the Master's service. He has won untold men and women to Christ in his quiet, unassuming way and has ever been an example for the young manhood of his community to follow. To his family he was always loving and patient. Striving to make a good living for them, and to rear them in the fear and admonition of the Lord. He was ever mindful of the gracious care and concern his wife felt for him, and showed his regard and appreciation of her often before his friends and church members. Because of his many virtues and the consistent Christian life he lived before his family, his children were early won to the Lord. He has been the right-hand man of our pastor, Rev. _____, who pays tribute to him today both as a personal friend and a brother in Christ.

Brother _____ was ever true to his high office as deacon of _____ Church. He was ever mindful of the charge which Paul gave to Christian deacons in the third chapter of 1 Timothy: "Likewise must the deacons be grave, not double-tongued, not given to wine, not greedy of filthy lucre: holding the mystery of the faith in a pure conscience, And let these also first be proved; then let them use the office of a deacon, being found blameless. Let the deacons be the husbands of one wife, ruling their children and their own house well. For they that have used the office of a deacon well, purchase to themselves a good degree, and great boldness in the faith which is in Christ Jesus."

Because Brother _____ lived up to his high commission of the deacon's manifold tasks as expressed by the apostle Paul, we know that today in his heavenly home he has already received that higher degree — that "good degree," Paul mentions. Although we miss him we realize that our loss is heaven's gain.

He has not served who gathers gold,

Nor has he served whose life is told

In selfish battles he has won

Or deed of skill that he has done,

But he has served who now and then
Has helped along his fellow men.

❧

Obituary for a Young Child

In an old English churchyard there is this inscription: "'Who plucked that flower?' cried the gardener, as he walked through the garden. His fellow servant answered, 'The Master!' And the gardener held his peace."

It is God's own sweet will that we turn away from our sorrow and go on with reverent earnestness to the new duties that await us. Standing and weeping over the grave where our little one is buried cannot bring back that which we have lost. When David's child was dead, he dried his tears and went at once to the house of the Lord and worshipped saying, "Can I bring him back again? I shall go to him, but he shall not return to me." He turned his eyes forward toward the glory in which his child was waiting for him, and began with new ardor to press toward that home. He turned all the pressure of his grief into the channels of holy living. This is the way every believer must learn to deal with his sorrows. Weeping inconsolably beside a grave can never give back love's vanished treasure, no matter how innocent and tender, nor can any blessing come out of such sadness.

God's garden had need of a little flower,
It had grown for a time here below,
But in tender love He took it above,
In a lovelier garden to grow.
It might have been marred had he left it below,
Although we had tended with care,
Had tilled and watered and hedged about,
Watching each petal fair.

There with His smile for the sunbeams
It will grow to perfection of bloom,

59

No withering blight or destructive storm
To crush out its sweet perfume.
Perhaps, sometimes, in the quiet hours,
We shall notice its sweet perfume
Steal softly down from the heavenly place,
'Till it seems to fill the room.

Then the earthly spot will seem less bare
As we think of the time to come,
When we shall enter the garden fair,
And find our transplanted bloom.

⟋⟋⟋

Obituary on the Passing of a Christian Father

We wish we could put into words the very real sense of loss that we experience personally in the homegoing of Brother _____, as well as the deep sympathy that we feel for each one of you in the loss of your devout and devoted Christian father, husband, and provider. Because we have seen the power of his Christian testimony in our church and all its organizations, we can easily imagine what bulwark of Christian strength he must have been to you in the family.

In times of indecision or uncertainty you must have looked to him for guidance and spiritual power, and now his very absence leads you to look above for guidance directly from your heavenly Father, who doeth all things well. When, without warning, a dear parent is called to his heavenly home, we feel at first so alone and friendless, but how clearly God will make you aware of His goodness in the days and years that are to come. How relieved you will be soon to know that there is no pain or sorrow that comes that will ever touch him again! While grief is so fresh and the sense of loss so keen, it is not always easy to learn, "Lean not to thine own understanding," but our gracious Lord and Savior will make the lesson clear to you if you look up to Him in faith.

One of the many reasons your beloved Father and our beloved brother in Christ will be so sorely missed is his power to encourage others in the work of the Lord. Often when his co-workers would be disheartened by lack of interest, or passing failure, he would remind them that God never demands success — only faithfulness to His cause. How often, in his prayers for his co-workers, he would call them, one by one, by name, and pray so intelligently for their needs that his prayers would do more good for his hearers than many a sermon, to say nothing of the divine power set in motion on their behalf.

Yes, we shall all miss him, none so sorely as you dear ones there in the home. To each of his friends he was the Christlike example and the confidence-inspiring, always-encouraging counselor and minister to our needs. How good God is to His children to give us such shining personalities as your father was. May God comfort and sustain you in this great loss and make you know Him as the "God of all comfort." "Thou wilt keep him in perfect peace whose mind is stayed on thee, because he trusteth in thee."

If Brother _____ had a creed other than to love and serve his Lord and Savior, it must have been something like this:

If I had but one year to live;
One year to help; one year to give;
One year to love; one year to bless;
One year of better things to stress;
One year to sing; one year to smile;
To brighten earth a little while;
One year to sing my Maker's praise;
A year to fill with work days;
One year to strive for a reward
When I should stand before my Lord,
I think that I would spend each day,
In just the very self-same way
That I do now. For from afar
The call may come to cross the bar

61

At any time, and I must be
Prepared to meet eternity.
So if I have a year to live,
Or just a day in which to give
A pleasant smile, a helping hand
A mind that tries to understand
A fellow-creature when in need
'Tis one with me — I take no heed:
But try to live each day He sends
To serve my gracious Master's ends.

ᏗᏬᏇᎲᎳ

Obituary for a Christian Mother

"Peace I leave with you, my peace I give unto you" (John 14:27). "Let not your heart be troubled" (John 14:1).

_____ was a devoted wife and mother, one who always put the interests of her family first, who saw to it that her children were given the best she could provide, in loving care, spiritual nourishment, and material comforts. The example she lived day by day will ever be a goal for her family to strive to reach. She was faithful to her church, always present at every service unless providentially hindered from being there, and saw to it that the family group attended with her.

The memories we have of _____ will always be dear to our hearts. We should not mourn her passing, but should rejoice for our departed friend has gone, we know, to a home more beautiful than any we have ever known. She gave her all for Him and for the family he gave to her, and now she is added to His great and blessed family in the world beyond our vision which for lack of a better name, we call Heaven.

"Yea, though I walk through the valley of the shadow of death, I will fear no evil: for Thou art with me; thy rod and thy staff they comfort me" (Psalm 23:4).

We express concern and sympathy for the children left without a mother, the man left without a wife, and beg them to turn their hearts toward God who does all things well, and who will be a mother to the motherless and will comfort all who mourn.

✧

Obituary for a Woman Who Has Been a Faithful Church Worker

"And God shall wipe away all tears from their eyes; and there shall be no more death, neither sorrow, nor crying, neither shall there be any more pain" (Revelation 21:4).

_____ was born in _____ (year) and died at _____ o'clock on _____ (date). She became a Christian when a very young girl and began her work in Christ's kingdom in _____ Church and has been a faithful and ardent worker for many years.

She was especially loyal to the work of the _____ (missionary society or other church auxiliary) never refusing a task because she was already too busy, or because she was too tired.

Today we are silent to pay tribute to a person who has lived among us as "one who went about doing good" and who always put Christ first in everything she did. During her months of illness she leaned heavily on the Lord, calling upon Him to help bear the pain when many times she could have called upon her loved ones, but refused to do so, knowing they were already tired and over-burdened.

_____ was a lovable character, a person everyone chose to have as a friend and willing to be a friend to all. She never pushed herself forward, but always stayed in the back-ground working, praying and doing whatever she was called upon to do for her Master.

"There's an open gate at the end of the road
Through which each must go alone
And there, in light we cannot see,
Our Father claims His own.

63

Beyond the gate your loved one finds happiness and rest
And there no comfort in the thought that a loving
God knows best."

❧☙

Obituary for a Church Member

Again death has visited us at _____ Church and taken from us for a little while a person who has set an example worthy for all of us to follow.

On occasions like this it is hard to put into words the deep feeling we have had for one who was beloved by all who knew him.

Today we have all stopped our regular work to pay tribute to _____ for what he has done to make this a better world to live in. He had no fear, for he knew his Lord so well and knew that He would take care of him all the way. What power our Lord has in time of trouble, and how wonderful it is to lean on Him when there is no one else who understands how deep is our grief.

He was converted _____ (date) in _____ Church and was baptized _____ (date). He took his place in our church, working faithfully for _____ years. He was known for always accepting whatever job was given to him whether large or small when he considered it a task for the furtherance of God's kingdom.

A life lived as _____ lived cannot die, but will live on in the hearts, memories, and ideals of all those who knew and loved him.

❧☙

Obituary for a Faithful Sunday School Teacher

We have gathered here together today to mourn the passing of Sister _____. She was born in _____ (year), was converted _____ (year), joined the _____ church and was baptized by _____.

The angel has visited our church again and taken from us a dear sister who has served our church and Sunday school for

_____ years. She will ever be near us, though unseen. She served her Lord and her people with a beautiful Christian life; her influence will always live in the lives of those she taught. Now as our hearts are saddened we feel that we cannot find one who could take her place of leadership, yet she was an ardent believer in the truth found in Psalm 73:24-25, "Thou shalt guide me with thy counsel, and afterward receive me to glory. Whom have I in heaven but thee? and there is none upon the earth that I desire beside thee."

Many people look upon death as a sad occasion. But the death of a Christian is a glorious time, for our Lord and Savior has said so, and the psalmist in Psalm 116:15 says, "Precious in the sight of the Lord is the death of His saint."

Sister _____ was a good neighbor, a loving mother, an inspiring, well-prepared, sacrificial teacher in our Sunday school, and above all a true Christian. She has worked hard, and now she has gone to be at rest:

Beloved, "It is well!"
Though deep and sore the smart,
The hand that wounds knows how to bind
And heal the broken heart.

Beloved, "It is well!"
Though sorrow clouds our way,
'Twill only make the joy more dear
That ushers in the day.

Beloved, "It is well!"
God's ways are always right,
And perfect love is o'er them all
Though far above our sight.

Beloved, "It is well!"
The path that Jesus trod,
Though rough and strait and dark it be
Leads home to heaven and God.

It is well with Sister _____. Her life was full and running over with good spirit; she was a happy person and seemed to enjoy every minute of her Spirit-filled life. She was never happier than when serving her Lord in her church and Sunday school.

Her years of teaching in the _____ department and her influence there have brought many into the house of the Lord. Now, it is time for us to take up where she left off and carry on in the way she has taught us. "Be ye doers of the Word, and not hearers only." She believed that one who was willing to work for the Lord would have everlasting bliss, and we know that her faith and her works are laid up as a memorial for her before God.

❦

MISCELLANEOUS ADDRESSES

Presenting a Pastor's Wife to a Gathering

Ladies and Gentlemen:

This, to me, is a very happy moment, and I feel keenly the signal honor given me to perform the task assigned. It is said that, back of every great man there is a great woman. It is my task at this time to present to this cosmopolitan gathering a noble woman. She is noble because of the noble virtues that emanate from her.

First of all, she is a Christian woman, possessed with the spirit of kindness, friendliness, and fellowship. Since coming among us these short months, by her tact of leadership, manifested interest in our welfare and advancement, she has already endeared herself to us, and we feel especially blessed of the Lord in having her one among us and one with us.

She, of whom I speak, is none other than the fine wife of our honorable pastor, Mrs. _____. Will you kindly stand and receive her?

❦

An Expression of Sympathy

To _____

It is with deep sympathy and tenderness of heart that we, your friends and co-laborers in Christ, send you these words to express to you, in a feeble way, our sincere sympathy for you in the death of your beloved _____; we are hoping that they will in some degree give you comfort and cheer in such dark hours as these which are yours at this time.

The passing of your _____ is the will of God, and yet there is a human tie that has been broken that bleeds the heart in agony and pain.

You must find comfort and consolation in the words of the apostle Peter, who said: "Cast your burdens on Him because He cares for you" (1 Peter 5:7).

Lift up your head and be strong, knowing you did what you could for his comfort, ease, and peace, until the end. God saw and He knows, therefore, we commend you to Him, who is able to comfort and cheer, and will dry your tears and heal your broken heart if you will put your unwavering faith in Him.

Your co-laborers are praying for you; you must also pray, for time and prayer will bring you relief. Make God your hope and look up to the hills from whence cometh your help. May God bless you and give you strength and courage.

Sympathetically yours, _____

❧❦❧

The Christian's Surrender Pledge

Today I give my life to Jesus Christ. I gladly acknowledge Him as my Lord and Master, my Savior, and my Friend.

I shall strive from day to day to love Him, to trust Him, and to serve Him. That I may better attain these high purposes, as I rely upon the Holy Spirit to give me strength, I pledge:

First, to observe a period of private prayer and devotion each day.

Second, to encourage family worship in my home.

Third, to read and study my Bible.

Fourth, to attend the services of my church unless prevented by sickness or causes that would be acceptable to an enlightened Christian conscience as reasons for absence.

Fifth, to accept cheerfully any call that comes to me for Christian service.

Sixth, to witness for Christ each day that I live, wherever I am, by word and by deed, and as the Holy Spirit leads me, to strive to win others for Christ.

Seventh, to contribute regularly of my means, according to my ability, to the financial program of my church. These things I promise. Help me, dear Master, to do them.

Signed: _____ Date _____

Short Address to Be Delivered at an Annual
Church Homecoming or Special Occasion

Master of Ceremonies:

This hour is the long-looked-for hour. With a deep-seated anticipation, we have looked forward to this annual celebration. For several years, this has been a glorious day in the religious and social life of this historic church, and every interest has been pointed in this direction.

Our affair — our annual homecoming is the highlight of this festival; take this out of the picture and there would be no need for this celebration.

This very unique, dignified, and beautiful occasion presents an ocular demonstration of the noble taste, religious and social tone of the members and pastor of this great church.

This occasion is deep in our affections because it brings afresh into our minds the life work of many of those who once were co-laborers here with us. We remember them in our midst, hand-in-hand, pressing forward towards the mark of the higher calling in God through our Lord Jesus Christ.

We remember them for their noble lives, lovable dispositions, and spiritual fellowship.

We hope and pray that each of you will enjoy this affair and open the doors of your hearts for the intake of everything good that may happen, that the magnanimity of this occasion will sweeten your souls with the abiding fervor of Christian fellowship.

This is your affair; it is for your enjoyment; and forget not that Christ is to be glorified in all that we may do.

ᴄᴏᴏᴏ

A Message for the Usher Board: An Exalted Position

"I had rather be a doorkeeper in the house of
My God, than to dwell in the tents of wickedness."

The above quotation expresses the sentiment in David's heart while king of Israel; and truly, this quotation bespeaks a deep-seated joy and solemn appreciation for an opportunity to be an Usher at the door of the Lord's house.

Usher, says Webster, means — "a doorkeeper; an officer who introduces strangers or walks before persons of rank; to escort," etc. However, Webster's definition is broad and made to cover any place or meeting; but the kind of usher David refers to is he who serves in the work of the Lord.

Think of the noble position and the golden service enjoyed by being an usher in things religious. No service rendered in the Lord's house should be regarded as small or unimportant, and when one has the distinctive privilege and signal honor to serve as an usher in the Lord's house, he or she should with bowed heads in humble humility say, "I thank the Lord."

Opening the door and admitting people into God's house, is more important than being a marshal at the door of Congress, or butler at the President of the United State's office. Opening the door, and walking before human beings down the aisles to secure a seat in God's house, is akin to the divine.

My friends, to each of you who serve in such capacity, I entreat to be proud of your position, prove yourselves worthy of the confidence your church has placed in you. Fill your places with dignity, and serve with joy and gladness, because you are serving in God's house. David said: "I would rather be a

69

doorkeeper in the house of my God, than to dwell in the tents of wickedness" (Psalm 84:10).

cᴏꙮꙨ

Appreciation Message for Workers Who Have Served Many Years in Sunday School

I want to express appreciation to those who have faithfully and loyally served and taught in our Sunday school for many years.

(Here read names of those who have worked, five, or ten, or more years in the school).

There are others who are not now teaching who have had long records of service to this school in the past. Not only our congregation but many men and women scattered far and wide are grateful for these and many other teachers who have sought to help boys and girls to build a firm spiritual basis on which to shape their lives. There is nothing more important than this first foundation. As we grow older, and usually when it is too late to let them know, we discover how much we owe to those who tried during the formative years of our childhood to help us build enduring foundations. We thank God for their patience with us, for their desire to help us, for their fine example of Christian character, which they gave us willingly and without pay, and which have set standards of life we have never forgotten.

We may have wandered away for some years, but how often when our children are growing up we realize as we watch them what the church and the Sunday school brought into our lives. We want them to have that same background, without which every child, no matter how rich materially, is poor.

We are grateful, therefore, to our Sunday school teachers, those of our own church and those in other churches across the world, those who throughout the years have been faithful witnesses to Him through teaching His Word and helping students to know Him as Savior and Lord. Quietly and unselfishly, with no fanfare of trumpets, or roll of drums, they have gone about their task week after week and year after year without asking or expecting personal credit or gain, and often getting none except the inner joy which comes to those who have not been disobedient to the heavenly vision.

We thank God for all who have helped us to learn more of the written Word and the Living Word. On behalf of our children we again say "thank you."

NOTES